The Secret Life of
A GARDEN

STEPHEN DALTON

The Secret Life of
A GARDEN

with Bernardine Shirley Smith

BCA

LONDON · NEW YORK · SYDNEY · TORONTO

This edition published 1992
by BCA by arrangement with
Ebury Press, an imprint of
The Random Century Group Ltd

CN 6339

This book was designed and produced by
Calmann & King Ltd, London

Designer: Richard Foenander
Printed in Singapore by Toppan Ltd

Stephen Dalton would like to thank Dr Arthur
Picton and Michael and Barry.

FRONTISPIECE: Hedgehogs (*Erinaceus
europaeus*) feed on insects, slugs, snails
and earthworms, and often wander about
the lawn at night. They spend the day in
nests of leaves under hedges or woodland
thickets. In winter they hibernate: their body
temperature drops to between two and six
degrees centigrade, and their respiration
slows down to about ten breaths per minute.
With the exception of the northern part of
Scandinavia, hedgehogs are found
throughout Europe. Those that live in Eastern
Europe have white, instead of brown, breasts.

Contents

Introduction

A garden only reveals its secrets to those who really look. To the silent, still observer much unfolds. Unfortunately, the pictures are fleeting, and even the keenest eye can only record an image momentarily. A disappearing tail, a flash of colour, a rapid wing beat may serve to arouse our curiosity, but cannot quench it. We look but we cannot see the hidden world of flora and fauna beneath the familiar pattern of lawn, flowerbed and trees. In the pages that follow, photographer Stephen Dalton hands us the key to the secrets of his garden. His camera captures movements too rapid for analysis by our limited vision and reveals details that would otherwise go unnoticed: the curious shapes and patterns of tiny plants such as liverworts, and the intricate structure of fungi and flowers. Like Lewis Carroll's Alice who discovered a wonderland down the rabbit hole, we are transported by the camera into another world. It is a world of unsuspected beauty and startling logic. It is a world which guards its privacy but, through the camera, we, the intruders, can observe its animal life from morning to night.

The history of the garden has been shaped by man's desire to create a sanctuary; to fulfil his dream of a perfect retreat. The idea of the Paradise Garden, which probably originated in Persia, has remained a dominant theme in much of the art, literature and poetry of gardens. Animals invariably feature in these ideal gardens. In the *Decameron* Boccaccio imagines animals living free in a garden, without fear of man. Medieval paintings depict enclosed, romantic gardens where roses can be seen rambling over arbours and pergolas. Animals are the most enchanting aspect of these paintings – birds perching among the roses and rabbits with huge ears and long legs.

In contrast, the gardens of the Renaissance were rigidly structured and outlined in clipped box or yew. An army of gardeners maintained the gravel-raked paths and neat parterres, so there was little opportunity for wildlife to settle. In England, in the eighteenth century, garden styles changed dramatically. It became fashionable among the gentry to have gardens 'improved'; transformed into landscaped parkland where creatures of field and woodland could be as much at home as they were in the wild. Lakes were dug and hills created in an attempt to imitate and rival nature; the park boundary was concealed so that there was no obvious division between garden and countryside. In time, deer were introduced and pheasants and other game birds encouraged.

Cottage gardens with their densely packed vegetable plots have always attracted animals, but by the beginning of the nineteenth century a social revolution was gaining impetus in the countryside. There was an exodus of people from farming and from the cottage craft industries of villages into the factories of the towns. The countryside was already becoming scarred by quarries, mines and factories, and criss-crossed by new channels of communication, roads, canals and railways. On the outskirts of the towns, comfortable villas housed the newly prosperous Victorian business- and tradespeople. Their gardens, fronted with wrought-iron railings and shrubberies, and planted with imported species such as rhododendrons, were often dark and forbidding. A monkey puzzle tree surrounded by a forlorn lawn, brightened by a bed of annuals, was not an inviting prospect for wildlife.

In contrast to these gardens, the stables and numerous outbuildings provided nesting places for swallows, swifts and martins, and holes for bats to hide and rest in by day. Rodents could raid the grain store, and white doves were a popular feature of the stable yard. The Victorian kitchen garden provided the greatest attraction for wildlife: vegetable plots were visited by numerous animals and by pests which were difficult to control. The Victorian author and illustrator Beatrix Potter made these creatures the subject of her stories for children: many people have grown up with a vivid picture of Mr McGregor chasing Peter Rabbit from the garden.

Today, as land continues to be swallowed up for industrial use and to accommodate an ever-increasing urban sprawl, the flora and fauna of the countryside are under threat. As their habitats disappear, animals are forced to seek refuge in our gardens. Modern agricultural practices, including the use of pesticides and weedkillers, and the uprooting of hedgerows, have destroyed many natural sources of food. Birds, for example, are forced to rely increasingly on the garden bird-table for their survival, particularly in the harsh winter months. Fortunately, there is now a greater awareness of, and sympathy for, the plight of wildlife. There is less indiscriminate use of poisons and pesticides, and the creation of wild-flower gardens is becoming a popular pursuit in response to a concern for plants in the wild.

Ecologically, Stephen Dalton's garden cannot be viewed in isolation. Around it there are various natural or semi-natural habitats: woodland, hedgerow, ponds, rough grassland and meadow. The woodland is ancient oakwood and is particularly rich in flora and fauna. Animals and plants from these habitats continually invade the garden. Insects, birds and mammals arrive seeking a new home or just visiting, and seeds germinate where they are not wanted. The family have devoted time and energy to establishing a nature reserve around the garden in which wildlife can not only survive but thrive, without threat from pollution, pesticides, herbicides, tree felling, land drainage, trapping or any other intrusion by man.

Each of the major habitats outside the garden supports well-established communities. In ecological terms, a community is a group of organisms living in the same habitat which depend on one another. Each animal population depends on an adequate food supply, space for movement and sites for homes or nests; plants depend on adequate light, a fertile soil and space for seeds to germinate. It is the interaction between the various populations which maintains the delicate balance within a community. For example, given enough light, plants make food in such abundance that there is plenty to spare for herbivores, which are in turn sufficiently numerous to provide food for predators. A simple food chain would involve field voles eating grass and in turn being eaten by owls. A more complex one might involve aphids sucking the juice from rose shoots, then being eaten by lacewings, which are eaten by spiders, which in turn provide food for shrews, which are then hunted by owls. Food chains are seldom this long or so simple, however. One food chain cannot be viewed in isolation. Aphids, for example, are also eaten by many other insects besides lacewings, and by birds. Eggs and larvae have their place in the food chains, and omnivores, scavengers, decomposers and parasites have to be considered too. In fact, one food chain is merely a strand in a vast food web which depends totally on the sun's energy. The implications of breaking one link in the web are serious. If gardeners could have one wish granted, to kill all aphids, the disruption of the food web would not only destroy the ecological balance of gardens, but could also be catastrophic for the habitats surrounding them.

In the garden itself there are a variety of specialized microhabitats, the most notable of which are the walls. These range from damp, shaded, stone walls to the bare, white, exposed walls of the house. The former supports many colonies of plants and animals: in its numerous crevices, mosses, liverworts and lichens grow and snails, slugs and woodlice hide. But the latter can only provide a home for spiders and for nesting house martins. The wooden boards of the garden shed, the eaves of the barn, the terrace steps, garden fence and the banks of the pond each provide a niche in which living organisms can survive. These microhabitats are too small and too specialized to sustain an ecologically balanced community of their own, but each supports colonies of plants and animals which contribute to the integrated community of the ecosystem as a whole.

Gardening inevitably involves some interference with the natural order, which in turn upsets the ecological equilibrium. Under natural conditions soil is seldom visible; the density of plants in the wild is sufficiently high to cover the ground. In a garden bed, whether flower or vegetable, planting is at a lower density in order to give plants space to grow and spread out. The ground may be cleared on more than one occasion each year, leaving the soil exposed and this gives weeds an opportunity to establish themselves. Moreover, the variety of plants in a cultivated flower or vegetable bed is much less than in the wild. There is sometimes even a monoculture, as in the rosebed or potato patch, so garden pests are attracted by a readily available meal. With the pests come viruses and fungi. The balance of nature has been disturbed and the garden becomes a battleground where the gardener fights weeds, pests and diseases.

All gardens are man-made and this garden is no exception. It is not a pretentious garden and makes no claim to fame. 'Gardens are for people, not for plants': it is from this premise that the garden has developed – its purpose is to please its owners. The house is situated high on a slope so the garden falls gently away to the woods and fields beyond. The plain wooden fence made from local sweet chestnut somehow links the garden with the surrounding countryside. The landscaping is semi-natural: with the exception of the terrace, no formal design has been imposed on the garden. The steep wall below the terrace and the steps leading down to the lawn are softened by plants and shrubs. Climbers spill over the terrace wall, cascading down to form a dark, damp, secret environment beneath, where toads, slugs, snails and earwigs live. Colour is provided by the herbaceous border; here the native geranium or cranesbill with its pastel-coloured flowers predominates from May to September.

Flowering shrubs, climbing roses and honeysuckle not only decorate the garden but also attract insects. Here and there one comes across an unusual plant, but this is decidedly not a plant collector's garden. The heather bed is an unexpected feature because the soil in the rest of the garden is not of the acidic, peaty kind which most heathers need. The bed has been artificially created to provide a totally different ecological niche. The tiny, bell-shaped flowers of heather are particularly attractive to bees; the acidic soil discourages earthworms and snails, but ground beetles and wolf spiders thrive here. Only one other feature has been artificially introduced and that is the pond. Partly secluded, it is there not merely for its aesthetic qualities but for its ecological interest. Many of the garden's amphibian and insect inhabitants – the toads and frogs, the dragonflies, mayflies, damselflies, mosquitoes and midges – lay their eggs in the pond and their young complete the first stages of their life cycles here. At the water's edge, plants such as liverworts, mosses and ferns thrive.

Not all the animals and plants which invade the garden are encouraged. It is something of a mystery why some plants are acceptable in a garden, while others are not tolerated. Although we may harbour nostalgic memories of buttercup meadows and pastures star-studded with daisies, these plants are weeded out of a garden. Some plants cannot be categorized, however: spring flowers, including primroses, forget-me-nots and bluebells, are as at home in this garden as they are in their wild habitats.

Particular plants growing on the other side of the garden fence persuade some of the more discriminate insect feeders to eat outside the garden. Clumps of stinging nettles in sunny positions provide leaves for caterpillars of the small tortoiseshell butterfly, the peacock and the red admiral. The purple flowers of common buddleia growing in the garden lure the emerging butterflies back over the fence to feed on nectar. Outside, charlock and mustard nurture caterpillars of the green-veined white. Jack-by-the-hedge and lady's smock supply caterpillars of the orange-tip, while the larvae of the brimstone feed on buckthorn. Unfortunately, snails and slugs cannot be persuaded to feed exclusively out in the wild as their homes are often difficult to locate.

With these exceptions, the garden welcomes visitors on wing or on foot. There is a special pleasure and excitement to be had in watching garden visitors, a sense of privilege that the robin perching on a garden spade or the hedgehog that comes out in the evening for a saucer of milk have chosen to share the garden and place their trust in man.

In the course of a day, subtle changes transform the garden. The rising and setting of the sun controls light intensity and temperature, and brings about changes in humidity. So, as the day progresses, the light becomes brighter then fades, the temperature rises then falls, and the air becomes drier before noon, only to become moist again by evening. These variations in climate greatly influence activity in the garden, which, though it often goes unnoticed by the casual observer, continues day and night. In the morning, at midday and in the evening, new, and often surprising, facts about the garden's inhabitants unfold.

Morning

Daybreak and nightfall, waking and sleeping are accepted as part of the natural order. Morning, noon and evening mark out the pattern for each day; the diurnal rhythm which is taken so much for granted. Daybreak is greeted in spring by the dawn chorus. The early rising of the sun prompts birds to find and secure for themselves a territory within which to build a nest and rear their young. This territory is then proclaimed in full voice to the waking world. On cold winter mornings the bird-table is a scene of great activity. The house sparrow has become a redoubtable acrobat, competing with the tit family for suspended nuts and lumps of fat.

Morning is the best time to see birds in the garden; while the earth remains damp, blackbirds can search for earthworms, wireworms and other grubs. Thrushes, besides seeking worms, ferret out snails that have not yet hidden themselves. A more unobtrusive bird is the dunnock or hedge sparrow which, like the wren, can be detected quietly searching under bushes for insects and their

The countryside surrounding the garden is rich in Wealden wildlife and plants. A **rabbit** (*Orictolagus cuniculus*) in the nearby meadow, sensing danger, stretches up above the long grass and bluebells to watch and listen for anything suspicious (right).

larvae to carry to its young. The garden not only provides birds with insects, grubs, snails and spiders but also weed seeds and, above all, berries. For those birds that can eat them, holly, rowan, hawthorn and pyracantha can supply a life-saving meal on a winter morning. The garden and its outbuildings also provide ideal nesting sites, but this has its disadvantages: hungry or greedy magpies and jays which prey on the eggs and young of small garden birds arrive in the early morning when there is less chance of their being seen from the house and chased away.

Gardens are not complete if not wakened to the sleepy cooing of a pair of wood pigeons, probably paired for life. The cock pheasant is also an early morning riser and struts into the garden alone, ignoring his harem of hen birds. The big attraction is the pond where a treat such as rush seeds or grubs may be found among the bog-dwelling plants.

Early morning is the time when most nocturnal mammals are retiring for the day, but the house mouse will often remain up and about. Although it is not welcome in the house, it happily takes up residence in the garden shed, barn or even under a hedge. Closely related is the brown rat, which will eat almost anything. Usually described as vermin, it can do the gardener a service by consuming weed seeds such as dock, goose-foot and fat hen.

Some plants literally seem to 'wake up' in the morning; their flowers close up in the evening, probably to protect the delicate inner reproductive parts during a cold, damp night, and then re-open in the morning. Daisies unfold their petals as the light intensity increases with the rising sun. Crocus flowers and tulips only open when the warmth of the sun's rays stimulates growth in cells on the inner surface of the petals, forcing them to bend outwards. At night, as the temperature falls, growth is faster on the outer surface, causing the petals to bend inwards once more.

Plants with trifoliate leaves, such as three-leaved clovers and wood sorrel, open up from a tightly folded 'sleep'. As the sun rises, special cells at the base of the leaflets respond to an increase in temperature and probably to an increase in light intensity. These cells fill with water, becoming turgid, plump and strong, so causing each of the three leaflets to unfold. The reason for this behaviour is not obvious; one explanation may be that the tightly folded leaf is more frost-proof.

Insects can be found resting motionless in the early morning, relying on camouflage or shelter for protection. It is only later that they begin to move about and gently unfold their wings. The male orange-tip butterfly is conspicuous with its wings outstretched, but when folded at rest the green-and-white-patterned underwing merges with the background of the green and white flowers on which the butterfly rests. Ill-served in this respect is the holly blue butterfly which lacks

Mammals and birds are most active in the garden in the early morning before man intrudes on the scene. It is always a pleasure to wake up to the rich song of the **song thrush** (*Turdus philomeles*) resounding through the countryside on a spring morning. This one pauses for a moment in a cherry tree before resuming its search for food.

Gardens are ideal habitats for song thrushes, especially if they are abundant in insects, slugs, snails, fruits and berries, and contain hedges or thick shrubbery for nesting.

good camouflage. This butterfly may be found resting near the pond. It actually drinks water from the edge of the pond, an uncommon practice among British butterflies which usually drink from the dew or raindrops on plants.

Around dawn the atmosphere surrounding the leaves of plants is very humid, and water from the leaves may not easily be evaporated. Uptake of water by the roots continues, however, and sets up a pressure causing droplets of water to exude from the tips of leaves – a process which is known to botanists as 'guttation'. Often mistaken for dew, these droplets can be seen hanging from the tips of blades of grass. In contrast, dew adheres to the blade of a leaf or collects in its saucer-shaped hollow.

Morning dew provides drinking water for many of the smaller animals and ensures a humid microclimate around plants throughout the morning. Dew tends to form during periods of high pressure on calm, clear nights which are usually followed by sunny days. The heat from the sun provides sufficient energy during the day to evaporate water from ponds, streams and plants. This water vapour is invisibly held in the air, but in the evening, as the temperature falls, a point is reached when the air is saturated and can hold no more. This is the dew point. If the ground temperature then falls below the air temperature, tiny droplets of water condense as dew on the ground and on plants. The droplets coalesce to form gleaming pearl-like globules. When frozen they form a hoar frost.

In winter the air temperature may fall below freezing point and the water vapour held in the air condenses into tiny droplets which can remain suspended as supercooled droplets or freezing fog. These tiny droplets drift on to the windward side of trees, fence posts, gates or telephone wires to settle in feathery patterns as ice crystals or rime frost.

It is only when coated with frost or laden with dew that the intricate structure of an orb web constructed by the garden spider is readily visible. Slung between the stems of plants or in a doorway, it is supported by its main framework and radial strands, both of which are composed of plain, strong threads. The spiralling, concentric threads, dotted with viscous, sticky globules trap the hapless victim. On some mornings the grass and the bushes appear to be silver-spangled with the webs of *Linyphiid* spiders. The webs look rather untidy, like a tangle of threads, but basically their builders erect 'scaffolding' and then sling a 'hammock' across it. Clumsy insects such as frog-hoppers trip over the strands of the scaffolding and fall into the hammock.

The neater web of the nursery web spider is not a trap but a tent-like home for the young. The female, being a wolf spider, hunts alone in broad daylight and so

Garden sheds attract a multitude of creatures, which make their homes in and around pots and boxes. This old vine- and peach-festooned shed provides shelter for robins, wrens, mice, a toad and numerous insects and spiders.

is more readily noticed on a morning in summer. She is long-sighted and pursues her prey rather as a cat pursues a mouse, creeping stealthily at first, then making a dash before landing on her victim. It requires patience to observe such drama.

A walk in the garden before breakfast can give a gardener an unpleasant shock. Rose shoots are covered in greenfly and bean shoots in blackfly. It is not that these pests arrived during the night, but rather that there has been a population explosion. A winged female aphid landing on a tender young shoot can look deceptively harmless and does not attract attention. In fact she may not just be one aphid but three generations in one: a grandmother with both her daughters and grand-daughters inside her. The embryos themselves already have embryos developing within them.

The mass reproduction of aphid young requires nitrogen for the manufacture of body protein. Aphids suck plant juices which are low in nitrogen and rich in sugar. So, in order to obtain adequate nitrogen, they take in large quantities of juice and pass out the undigested part which is known as 'honey dew'. This is mainly sugar and makes the leaves very sticky. Ants are especially fond of honey dew and can be seen in constant procession up and down stems to harvest it.

Blue tits consume many aphids and rise early to select choice specimens. Rabbits, too, are up early nibbling grass. Only mammals and birds are up and about in the cool of the morning because they are the two groups in the animal kingdom that keep warm and active when the weather is cold. At one time referred to as 'warm-blooded' animals, they are now better described as 'endotherms'. As the term implies, their body warmth is generated from within, released from energy-rich food; as long as they can eat, they keep warm and their body temperature remains constant. They are completely dependent on finding food which acts as fuel for keeping warm. On a cold winter morning birds starved of food can be found dead and frozen stiff. A few mammals survive by hibernating and in some this adaptation actually allows their body temperature to be lowered to within a few degrees of that of the environment. Bats and hedgehogs are two garden animals who come into this category; they become torpid as if in a stupor and most certainly will not be active at dawn on a winter morning when other mammals and birds are beginning their search for food.

Nothing can quite compare with the peace of the garden in early morning, especially in summer. There is an air of expectancy, anticipation of the hustle and bustle to come. As the sun climbs higher in the sky, birds squabble, darting movements catch the eye and the garden comes alive with the humming and buzzing of insects.

Late in the summer some trees are already showing signs of the fall to come. The leaves of this **handkerchief tree** (*Davidia involucrata*) are colouring up as the pigments are broken down and nutrients are transported to the trunk for storage through the winter (right). The pigments which remain will give rise to the glorious hues of autumn.

Beyond the garden, the Weald of Sussex stretches out to the south, with the South Downs in the distance (overleaf). Rich in hedges and broad-leaved woodland, the area is an ideal habitat for a wide variety of plants and animals, a bonus for those who have gardens within its confines.

Few people are inclined to encourage **brown rats** (*Rattus norvegicus*) to their neighbourhood, but one or two can do little harm, and add variety to the life of the garden (below). Often found around water, rats, like most mammals, are strong swimmers. This one is exploring a drain which discharges into a pool of water.

The **house mouse** (*Mus musculus*) adds a new dimension to life around the house and potting shed (right). Like brown rats, house mice have spread from Asia to every part of the inhabited world. Although this mammal can be found in open countryside, it prefers to be close to man where food is easily available.

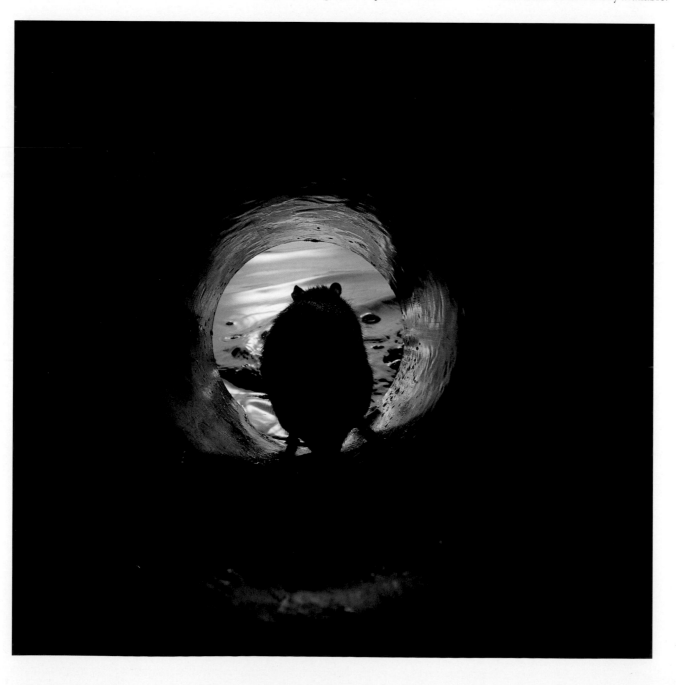

Coated with dew, a small patch of **red deadnettle** (*Lamium purpureum*) is growing in the shade of a katsuru tree. Most wild flowers have evolved their colour, form and scent as a means of encouraging potential pollinators, and the greater the variety of flowers grown in a garden, the more insects it will attract. Insects are vital for the ecology of a garden, providing food for mammals and birds. Patches of wild flowers in the grass or amidst the borders, therefore, not only enhance the beauty of the garden but do much to encourage wildlife.

Edged with droplets, the leaves of a **katsuru tree** (*Cercidiphyllum japonicum*) catch the morning light. This tree originates from the Far East and is noted for the variety of its autumn leaves.

In the early morning mists of autumn, a moisture-laden **orb web** built in a marsh thistle is conspicuous in the adjacent meadow (right).

The leaves, or fronds, of **ferns** are tightly coiled when young, and unwind as they grow and expand (below). Rather than producing seeds like familiar flowering plants, ferns reproduce by spores formed in structures called 'sori' on the undersides of the fronds.

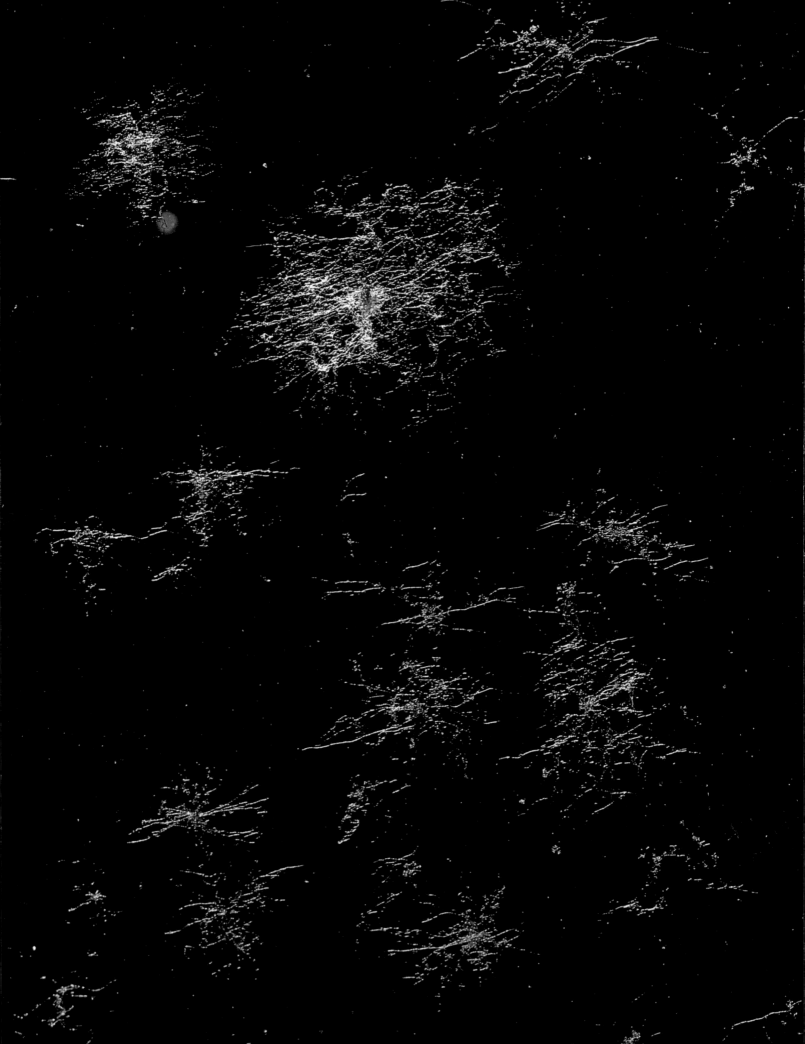

At high magnification the **fungus** *mycelium* is shown branching out from dust particles which have settled on a window pane of the garden shed (left). This 'mildew' can grow almost anywhere when conditions are sufficiently damp.

A late spring frost has decorated the flower and leaf edges of a miniature **rhododendron** (below).

Wood pigeons (*Columba palumbus*) are frequent visitors to town and country gardens (above). Food is always more difficult to find when there is frost or snow around; here a pigeon searches for morsels scattered from the bird-tray.

After a light fall of snow, a golden-leaved **yew** (*Taxus* sp.) is decorated with flecks of white (right).

To encourage both garden and wild bog-dwelling plants, such as irises, kingcups, forget-me-nots and primulas, water from a ditch has been routed to flood a small area (left).

A **wolf spider** (*Lycosidae* family) basks in the early morning sun (below). Unlike the majority of spiders, which trap their prey in webs, most wolf spiders lead a wandering existence, finding food by pouncing on any hapless insect which passes by.

One sure way of attracting wildlife to a
garden is to create a pond; even a
small one provides a home for a whole
new range of plants and animals. A pond is
also used by many non-aquatic creatures as
a feeding, drinking and washing area. Here
a cock **pheasant** (*Phasianus colchicus*)
struts round the water's edge, looking for a
suitable place to drink.

This young **common frog** (*Rana temporaria*) is almost ready to leave the pond where it has spent its life so far. The mortality rate of tadpoles and froglets is very high, as in the water they are preyed upon by dragonfly nymphs, water bugs and beetles, as well as by fishes, newts and birds. On land, the frog will be pursued by a host of new enemies.

34

One of the most attractive features of a garden is the range of leaf shapes and colours which can be found within a small area. All these leaves grow within a few feet of each other. **Japanese maples** (top and bottom), **lupins** (centre) and **geraniums** (right) provide cover and sometimes food for all kinds of animals.

However attractive a blanket of snow
may appear, birds have a difficult
time if it lies around for too long,
particularly in very cold conditions. Apart
from the physical difficulty of finding food
when the ground is covered and hard,
extra food is vital to keep birds and small
mammals warm in sub-zero temperatures.
Well-stocked food trays increase birds'
chances of survival.

   After a feed at the bird-tray, a **robin**
(*Erithacus rubecula*) conserves energy
by resting quietly in a cotoneaster bush
and puffing out its feathers for more
efficient insulation (above).

Starlings (*Sturnus vulgaris*) are not very popular with those who feed garden birds, as they descend in flocks to gorge themselves on food intended for smaller species (right). Gardeners should welcome them, however, as they probe the lawn for cranefly larvae (leatherjackets). As well as insects, worms and slugs, they eat fruit, berries and other vegetable matter.

The starling is an extremely adaptable and successful species, and has become very common in both town and country areas. It was introduced to New York in 1890 and by 1950 had colonized most of North America.

In cold weather **pheasants** (*Phasianus colchicus*) always take advantage of the bird-tray (above). Some are so tame that they occasionally walk into the house in the hope of cadging titbits.

The **wren** (*Troglodytes troglodytes*) is very adaptable in its choice of habitat; it may be found in woodland or reedbeds, or even on rocky islands and moorland. It survives well in gardens, particularly those that have dense vegetation. The bird's characteristic low, short flight from shrub to shrub soon betrays its presence, if its powerful warbling song or alarm calls do not do so first. To maintain its territory, the wren sings throughout the year.

The garden shed is a popular place for **house mice** (*Mus musculus*) to rear their offspring. The nest is usually tucked away in rags or sacking behind rarely used garden tools. The success of this species is due to its adaptability and capacity to breed prolifically. One mouse may produce several litters a year of between six and twelve blind, naked young which develop so quickly that they are capable of independence within a fortnight and able to breed after six weeks.

With autumn come the early morning mists, clothing everything in the nearby meadow in a thick deposit of dew. The meadow acts as a reservoir, supplying the garden with a range of wildlife it might otherwise lack.

Diving out of its nest box at an explosive speed, a **blue tit** (*Parus caeruleus*) sets off for the umpteenth time in search of caterpillars. Its numerous fledglings have a seemingly insatiable appetite: one brood may need between 500 and 1,000 caterpillars every day. When nesting close to woodland, the hen may lay up to fourteen eggs, but in gardens, where suitable food is often scarce, smaller clutches are more normal.

A large patch of **cranesbills** (*Geranium*) in the herbaceous border attracts a wide variety of bees and hover flies (left). There are around 300 species of these flowers, many of which can be found growing wild in Britain and Europe.

As the day warms up, a show of **daisies** (*Bellis perennis*) gradually unfurl their petals (below). Instead of using weedkillers and fertilizers on a lawn and mowing to within a quarter of an inch of the soil, it can easily be managed to encourage wildlife and to look more beautiful, attracting daisies, clover, speedwell, plantains, medick, self-heal and other low-growing flowers.

On mornings in early autumn the vast
number of spiders present in a
garden is revealed. Dew-laden **webs** of all
shapes and sizes stand out with exquisite
delicacy on each hedge, shrub and tuft of
grass in the first morning light.

Over the last few years the **holly blue** (*Celastrina argiolus*) has become much more common and is often seen in gardens with holly trees nearby. The butterflies of the first flight appear in April or May, and the female lays her eggs on the underside of flower buds. The larvae that hatch feed on the buds and young green berries. The adults fly in July and August.

Perched in the security of a cotoneaster bush, a **dunnock** or **hedge sparrow** (*Prunella modularis*) augments its more usual diet of insects with a breadcrumb found at the base of the bird-table (above). Rather than perching on bird-tables, this bird prefers to scavenge for food on the ground. Dunnocks are not in fact related to sparrows, being much closer to robins.

Chaffinches (*Fringilla coelebs*) are one of the most common birds in Britain (top right), although their population has declined since around 1960, probably due to the effects of agricultural chemicals. The bright and cheerful song of this often confiding little bird is very variable, differing noticeably from one part of the country to another.

A lawn is a favourite hunting ground for the **blackbird** (*Turdus merula*) (right). It can frequently be seen turning over dead leaves in its search for worms and insects. The clear, fluty song of this bird must be among the most beautiful sounds to be heard in the garden.

Greenfly and **aphids** are rarely encouraged, yet play a vital role in the ecology of garden wildlife, providing food for both insectivorous birds and the larvae of many attractive insects such as hover flies, lacewings and ladybirds.

Far from being scarce, the **scarce aeshna** or **migrant hawker** (*Aeshna mixta*), as it is variously called, is locally common in most seasons. Once a migrant from the Mediterranean, the species has extended its range northwards over the last fifty years and now breeds successfully in southern and eastern England.

Unlike other Aeshna species, the migrant hawker is not territorial when hunting insects, often flying high in the company of others. It is a lovely sight to see a dozen or so of these magnificent insects patrolling a clearing in the fading light of a warm summer's evening. This one has spent the night in the herbaceous border, resting on a plume poppy.

Often glimpsed flying jauntily down a country lane in early spring, the **orange-tip** butterfly (*Anthocharis cardamines*) also frequents gardens, especially those with nectar-rich wild flowers. The female likes to lay her eggs on lady's smock or garlic mustard. The orange-tip has two broods; the first appears on the wing during early spring and the second in late summer.

The dew-covered **hammock webs** which glisten on the lawn and hedges in autumn are made by money spiders (*Linyphiidae*), a family of spiders containing several hundred diminutive species of an eighth of an inch long. At this time of the year they are stirred into restless activity, cloaking the grass with criss-crossing filaments that shimmer in the light.

Plant and animal life around the water's edge is always fascinating and the exotic-looking **skunk cabbage** (*Lysichiton americanus*) is no exception (below). Huge leaves, sometimes over three feet long, surround the yellow spathe and greenish flower-bearing spadix, which has a disgusting smell.

Although the skunk cabbage is naturalized in a few parts of Europe, it originated in North America where it is found in swampy ground. It belongs to the largely tropical arum family (*Araceae*), the most familiar European species of which is the cuckoo pint or lords-and-ladies.

A thick coat of morning dew has formed on a **euphorbia fireglow** (*Euphorbia griffithia*) (left). This belongs to the spurges, a group of plants which contains evergreen and semi-evergreen shrubs, succulents and perennials, as well as annuals. The sap of these plants is thick and milky.

Silver beads of dew have covered every plant in the garden, including the blossom of the Bramley apple tree (below). Later in the day as the air warms up, some of the flowers will open, exposing their pollen and nectar to foraging insects.

This **honey bee** (*Apis mellifera*) is collecting pollen from the blossom (right). Hairs covering the bee's body trap the sticky pollen; later the bee combs the pollen into pollen baskets, seen here on the hind legs, before transporting it back to the hive.

Although the **elder** (*Sambucus nigra*) is one of our most common woody plants (above), there are good reasons to encourage its growth in gardens. Birds such as blackbirds, starlings, pigeons, robins and blackcaps can feast on the berries which are rich in vitamin C, while man can use the cream-coloured flowers for making cordials and wine.

A view of the garden from the terrace (right), looking south towards heather beds, azaleas and a magnolia growing at the side of the small pond.

Midday

At midday the sun has reached its peak in the sky, but this is not necessarily the hottest part of the day; in summer the temperature can continue to rise in the afternoon. Those animals which were searching for food earlier are now taking a siesta, leaving space in the garden for some of its other occupants to feed. These are the invertebrates, and some vertebrates, such as fish, amphibians and reptiles, all of which are directly dependent on heat energy from the sun to become active. Unlike birds and mammals, they have no internal regulating mechanism for controlling body temperature so they do not need to eat to keep warm. At one time they were known as 'cold-blooded'; this is not an accurate description because their blood is cold only when the environmental temperature is cold. As the day gets warmer, they too get warmer, and if the weather is very hot they are in danger of becoming overheated and must protect themselves in cool, moist shade. The more modern term 'ectotherm' better describes these animals as their bodies are heated from outside. This is an energy-efficient system; solar energy is provided naturally and there is little expenditure of energy when the temperature is low because the ectotherms are sluggish and inactive. Only as the

A **hover fly** (*Catabomba pyrastri*) sucks the nectar from a monkey flower growing by the pond (right). Hover flies (*Syrphidae*) are amongst the most attractive of flies, often strikingly marked in bright colours.

day gets warmer can they be seen soaking up the sun and in consequence become livelier. This explains why many of the animals that are busy around the garden at midday differ from those seen earlier.

Colour in the garden is intensified by the noon sunshine and enhanced by the butterflies which now fly from flower to flower. The origin of the pigments in a butterfly's wing is not fully known but they can hardly be equalled for sheer brilliance and variation in pattern. Green pigments are very rare in British butterflies, a curious fact considering the abundance of the green pigment chlorophyll in leaves, and the butterfly's need for camouflage. The green spattering on the underwing of the orange-tip is thought to be an optical effect resulting from a mixture of black and yellow scales.

The red admiral and the painted lady seem at home in an English garden, yet they are migrants and cannot truly be claimed to be British. The butterflies observed sunning themselves on the buddleia will have hatched out in early summer, very likely a second hatch. The adults might survive the winter by hibernating or they might be blown on the wind back to warmer climes. The small tortoiseshell and the peacock also frequent the garden. They too hibernate through the winter and need safe niches in the outhouses, garden shed or the hollow tree. The brimstone comes into the garden to hibernate in evergreen bushes, while the comma can actually survive the winter among undisturbed dead leaves. The white admiral is a woodland butterfly but has extended its territory to visit the garden.

Two common garden butterflies are the large white and the small white. At one time they would drift across the Channel from the Continent in clouds or swarms to lay their eggs. These would hatch into tiny green caterpillars that grew visibly larger as they devoured any cabbage crop. Since the introduction of pesticides, however, their numbers have decreased and their presence in the garden is less alarming as a result. The small copper has a lovely metallic sheen which is most noticeable as a band along the edge of the hind wing. Less conspicuous is the day-flying green longhorn moth. Its larvae are leaf miners; they bore tunnels through the leaves of trees such as the field maple, making meandering patterns on the leaf.

A familiar garden visitor, the bumble bee, is not inclined to sting. The honey bee is more feared, despite the fact that it unwittingly works for man, producing copious quantities of honey and pollinating many species of flowering plants. Of the two, the bumble bee has the longer tongue and can sip nectar from deep down inside tubular flowers such as foxgloves and red clover. The honey bee can exploit many sources of nectar and pollen but relies on man to keep the garden well

Despite persecution by man, the **magpie** (*Pica pica*) population seems to go from strength to strength, with many birds breeding in built-up areas where they are safe from gamekeepers. Magpies are catholic in their diet, feeding on invertebrates, small mammals, carrion, grain and fruit and, like the urban fox, they are becoming accomplished scavengers. Unfortunately, these crafty crows also raid the nests of song birds, taking eggs and fledglings, and frequently destroying almost every nest in the garden. Notwithstanding their failings, magpies are certainly attractive birds, and are tolerated in very small numbers in this garden.

stocked with flowers and, further afield, to grow clovers, beans and oil-seed rape. Notwithstanding the care and attention lavished on them, honey bees obey an instinctive urge to depart and seek a new home. On a warm summer afternoon they can be seen following their queen in a vast swarm.

Wasps elicit disagreeable feelings, perhaps because, like house-flies, they are not content to remain in the garden, but enter the house in search of food. Both are indiscriminate feeders. A house-fly will feed on practically anything, including dung, and so spreads disease. The common wasp is more discerning and is especially partial to sugar-rich foods. Unable to probe many flowers for nectar because its tongue is too short, it feeds on ripe fruit, but also on carrion and insects which it takes to its carnivorous larvae. The hover fly, which looks similar to a wasp, often pays the price of mistaken identity when it is destroyed by man. Its mimicry of the wasp does protect it from predators, however. It feeds solely on nectar, while its larvae feed almost entirely on aphids.

On a hot summer day a low chirping sound comes from the long grass at the edge of the garden. This is the mating 'song' of the male short-horned grasshopper. It can be heard in the middle of the day when it is very warm, unlike the noise of bush crickets which lasts all through long summer evenings. The grasshoppers can be found quivering in full sunlight on leaves or flowers – quivering because their vibrant sound is made by rubbing ridges on their legs along their wings.

The pond contributes in an indirect way to the colour of the garden at midday. Thirteen species of dragonfly have been recorded in the garden, their iridescent wings reflecting the colours of the rainbow. They are daytime hunters and depend on good vision for catching their prey on the wing. They consume many insect pests, and their young, or nymphs – greedy predators that feed on mosquito larvae – are the terror of the pond. Emerging from their final moult, dragonflies depend on the sun to dry out their wings.

Often seen in the pond is the large edible or water frog. A strong swimmer, it spends most of its time in the water, so is less of an ally to the gardener than the common frog which flicks out its long, sticky tongue to catch moving insects. During the brighter part of the day the pigment-containing cells in the frog's skin contract so that by evening it may appear paler in colour than in the morning. The milky secretion on its skin can be poisonous and is certainly protective. Snakes, however, are unaffected by this and are able to eat frogs with impunity. The grass snake is attracted into the garden by the pond and by the warm compost heap which acts as an incubator for hatching its eggs. By midday the snake has warmed up and feels pleasant to the touch, not cold or chill as is often imagined. It relies on

Although they are not encouraged by gardeners, the vivid yellow flower heads of **dandelions** (*Taraxacum officinale*) are popular with many insects. The greyish-white, spherical 'clocks' which follow consist of seeds and their hairy parachutes. When fully ripened, the seeds are wafted away by the wind.

energy from the sun to enable it to move, and moves fast when it is alarmed.

The squirrel is an early riser and is active on and off throughout the day. It is an irritable animal, prone to outbursts of bad temper, and 'swears' at intruders. In summer it eats fruit, seeds, leaves, shoots, flower buds, bulbs and roots, but in autumn its preference is for nuts, fruit stones and pips, and it will also eat some fungi. Most annoyingly, it has discovered a fast-food source at the bird-table.

Field voles have provided supplementary food for predators like the stoat since myxomatosis reduced the number of rabbits. Rabbits come out of safe hiding to feed in the early morning and evening, but a doe with young will venture out for an extra feed in the middle of the day. The stoat hunts by day and by night and will tackle a rabbit in broad daylight. Being much smaller than a rabbit, it is often invisible as it drags its limp prey back to its family.

While it is easy to observe animals feeding, the method by which plants make food, photosynthesis, is a far more secret process and one which took scientists a long time to research and elucidate. It is the process by which plants use the sun's energy to manufacture carbohydrates from two simple ingredients: carbon dioxide from the air and water from the soil. It is at its most efficient around midday when light intensity is at an optimum. In spring and summer the light intensity at midday is sufficient to sustain the maximum rate of photosynthesis, but by dusk the rate will be negligible. In autumn and through the dim, cold days of winter, the rate of photosynthesis is so slow that it is not worthwhile for most plants to keep their leaves. Food is stored in seeds, bulbs, tubers and roots to enable the plants to survive the winter, alive but dormant.

At midday plants face their most challenging problems. In summer this is the time when both temperature and light intensity are high, but it does not necessarily follow that humidity is also high. Unlike animals, plants cannot drink. They need water for photosynthesis but they have no control over its uptake. Water enters the roots by a process called osmosis and travels up the stem to the leaves. In bright sunshine the pores of the leaves are open to admit carbon dioxide and, unavoidably, water passes out. On a hot, dry day when water evaporates from the leaves faster than it enters the roots, the plants inevitably wilt. It is not a good idea to water plants in the middle of the day, however, because each water drop acts like a miniature lens, focusing heat rays from the sun on to one spot. This damages cells and causes a tiny blemish. It is far better to wait for the cool of the evening; as dusk falls the pores in the leaves close, preventing water loss, and the plant can then replenish its water store. Evening is eagerly awaited not only by wilting plants but by many animals which have been asleep through the heat of the day.

Introduced to England from North America about a hundred years ago, the **grey squirrel** (*Sciurus carolinensis*) has now all but replaced the red squirrel in most of the country (right). With its powerful hind feet the squirrel can make prodigious leaps from tree to tree. Its large, bushy tail helps balance, and when spread out laterally, the long tail hairs assist aerodynamic stability.

The garden pond is surrounded by verdant vegetation. Sprouting on an island of water lilies (overleaf) are **yellow monkey flowers** (*Mimulus guttatus*).

The most common visitors to the bird-tray are generally **blue tits** (*Parus caeruleus*) and **great tits** (*Parus major*), peanuts serving as an irresistible attraction (right). The two birds on the right of the feeder are great tits. The blue tit is predominantly powder blue in colour, whereas the great tit is larger and boldly marked in yellow and black.

During the day bird-tables are not only popular with birds, but also with mammals such as the **grey squirrel** (*Sciurus carolinensis*). At night other mammals, such as wood mice, may climb up and take food, while hedgehogs sometimes scavenge below.

An **edible frog** (*Rana esculenta*) soaks up the sun (left). Closely related to the common frog, the edible frog is not generally found in Britian. Attempts at introducing the species from the Continent have not been wholly successful, although there are a few small colonies in southern England. This particular edible frog has survived at least one winter in the pond.

As the pond is bounded by thick natural and cultivated vegetation (below), a variety of animals live concealed close to the water's edge. Among the creatures here are all kinds of water-loving insects, two species of frog and two species of newt. The pond is also visited by grass snakes and by many birds, including a heron, which has finally consumed all the fish.

There are often more bumble bees searching for nectar and pollen among the garden flowers than honey bees, particularly in cold or wet weather when honey bees tend to return to the warmth of the hive. This **bumble bee** (*Bombus*) is foraging at a lupin, its pollen baskets brimming with pollen (right).

Bumble bees have well-organized colonies and divide their labour, but their nests, which are usually underground, consist of far fewer individuals than those of honey bees. Unlike honey bees, only the queen survives the winter.

The bee's sense of smell and powers of colour discrimination allow it to recognize different flowers. This worker **honey bee** (*Apis mellifera*) is extracting nectar from the flower of a runner bean (right). Once it starts to visit a particular flower, the bee tends to continue to visit the same species for as long as the nectar or pollen is available.

The antennae of bees are sensitive to water vapour and can easily guide them to a small source (below). This is important because large amounts of water are needed to dilute the food of the brood. The hive has to recruit many foragers as water carriers.

The **jay** (*Garrulus glandarius*) is perhaps the most handsome member of the crow family, looking quite exotic at close quarters (above). Its favourite habitat is the oakwood, so it is not seen in the garden every day, though its harsh calls can often be heard echoing from the woods nearby. In autumn the jay feeds on acorns, storing those it cannot eat in the ground.

Many of the acorns not recovered take root and grow into saplings. This ensures the survival of both the jay and the oak, and is probably the most important method of oak-tree regeneration.

Jays also feed on other fruits, seeds and insects. In spring they raid birds' nests, taking the eggs and young; even chicken eggs are very acceptable if found.

All birds need to drink and wash, so a garden pond acts like a magnet, drawing in birds from a wide area. Due to the confined space on the rock island, the **great tit** (*Parus major*) and a **redpoll** (*Carduelis flammea*) engage in a territorial dispute (top right). The great tit soon wins the argument and proceeds to have a thorough wash (right).

Wherever there is a garden pond, the chances are that frogs will be living in long grass and other suitably moist places nearby. The **common frog** (*Rana temporaria*) does not use leaping as its normal means of locomotion, reserving the enormous power of its hind legs for escaping danger (right). It only takes about a tenth of a second for the legs to extend, propelling the creature up to twelve times its own length. To prevent damage to the cornea during this high-speed manoeuvre, the frog retracts, or in this case semi-retracts, its eyes.

It is always a privilege to have one's garden selected as a nesting site by a pair of **spotted flycatchers** (*Musciapa striata*). They are one of the last summer migrants to appear, arriving in mid-May and returning to Africa between July and October. The spotted flycatcher is essentially a woodland bird, but large gardens with mature trees and a good supply of flying insects, are perfectly suitable habitats. What makes this little brown bird so engaging is its manner of catching prey. It flutters out from a perch, often a dead branch or fence post, twisting and turning in the air in its effort to pursue and catch an insect, before returning to the same or to a nearby perch.

Flycatchers often nest amongst vegetation close to a tree trunk, garden wall or house, but can be encouraged to use open-fronted nest boxes.

One of the most thrilling events of the year occurs in spring when the **house martins** (*Delichon urbica*) arrive all the way from Africa to inspect their old homes under the eaves of the house (left). Although we know they spend winter in this vast continent, exactly where they go remains a mystery.

House martins are colonial birds, and the faint, soporific murmuring of contented young can be heard from a dozen or so nests round the house both day and night. Sadly, the left-hand nest has been taken over by house sparrows which ripped apart the entrance hole and discarded the martins' eggs.

During the heat of the day, myriads of minute **red mites** (*Acari*) run frenziedly in all directions over the warm bricks and walls of the house and terrace (below). When two meet, they usually have a brief 'wrestling' match before continuing with their hectic activities.

Mites are not insects, possessing eight legs and unsegmented bodies like spiders. The majority of mites are very small, almost on the limit of human vision.

Earthworms provide a rich source of food for a wide range of birds and mammals, as well as aerating the soil and transporting leaves and other vegetable matter into the soil. **Earthworm casts** are most common during autumn.

The **snake's head lily** or **fritillary** (*Fritillaria meleagris*) occurs naturally in the damp meadows and open woodland of northern Europe but, except where it has been introduced, it is rare in England. It can be grown in gardens where conditions are suitable.

On hot summer afternoons the sound of serenading **grasshoppers** (*Acrididae*) can be heard drifting from the meadow. Their buzzing tone is not so highly pitched as that of bush crickets. It is produced by rubbing the inside of the hind legs against hardened veins on the forewing. Grasshoppers can be differentiated from bush crickets by their much shorter antennae.

The **broad-bodied chaser** (*Libellula depressa*) is a very regular visitor to the garden pond, where it can be seen skimming over the surface. When laying eggs, it dips the tip of its abdomen into the water repeatedly. At other times it may just rest in the sun on its favourite twig or reed. The less common males, which are powder-blue in colour rather than yellow-brown, are extremely territorial, chasing away any other males which dare to venture too close.

An orange **fungus** (*Phlebia*) radiates out from an old sawn log (right). This is a common fungus found on the bark of dead deciduous trees at any time of year.

The garden supports a range of mammals, including two species of vole. Here the **field vole** (*Microtus agrestis*) feeds at the base of a rotten stump (below). Its favourite habitats are meadows and lush pastures, but it also frequents gardens, orchards and young plantations, where it feeds mainly on vegetable matter, supplemented with a few insects. In addition to burrowing underground, the field vole has a network of surface runs through the grass enabling it to creep or run along, in the hope of avoiding detection by predators such as the kestrel, its arch-enemy.

Robins (*Erithacus rubecula*) can become tame very easily, sometimes standing only a few yards away as insects and worms are turned up by the spade (below). They are very aggressive birds, frequently chasing one another away from their overlapping territories. They may be heard singing in most months of the year, and have an attractive warbling song in spring, which in autumn becomes slower and rather sad.

During late spring the **blossom** on the ornamental cherry is so profuse that its branches droop with the weight. A week or two later the petals float down to form a pink mantle on the lawn, where they rapidly shrivel and fade (left).

Being essentially a water-loving creature, the **grass snake** (*Natrix natrix*) is most likely to visit country gardens with ponds or streams close by (below). It lays its dozen or more eggs in warm, fermenting material to hasten incubation, so compost heaps are an added attraction for the female. The size of the grass snake varies considerably, exceptional specimens reaching a length of four or five feet in Britain, and up to eight feet in southern Europe.

It is always exciting to glimpse a rare garden visitor such as the **stoat** (*Mustela erminea*). As well as rabbits, the stoat (bottom) will hunt for fish, eels, mice and even moles. It moves in a series of undulating bounds.

The **pheasants** (*Phasianus colchicus*) which live in the garden are rarely seen flying, but spend most of the time lurking amongst the vegetation (right). On the few occasions a pheasant does become airborne, its performance is impressive. Short, stubby wings enable the bird to take off very rapidly, while a long tail helps it to weave in and out between trees.

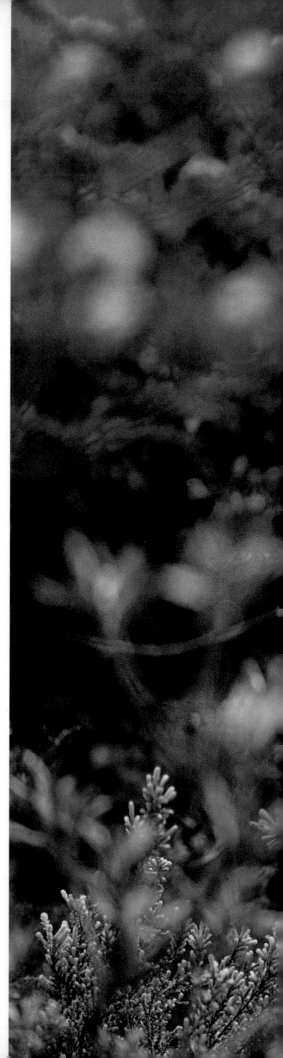

At the edge of the meadow a small group of **common spotted orchids** (*Dactylorhiza fuchsii*) regularly appears (below). There are about 30,000 species of orchids worldwide, the majority of which are tropical and epiphytic, growing on the branches and trunks of trees. Most species depend on a fungus for their survival.

A swarm of **honey bees** (*Apis mellifera*) have collected on the branch of an apple tree (left). When bees swarm, only a proportion of the colony leave the hive. By migrating in a swarm, complete with a new queen, the bees can establish a new home in fresh territory without much risk. It is a simple division of the colony at a time of prosperity.

Wasps may be irksome and even painful at times, but like so many unwelcome creatures they fulfil a useful function in nature. These **common wasps** (*Vespula vulgaris*) are feeding on the sweet juices from a fallen apple (right). They are clearly dominant over the flies.

Although adult wasps are fond of sweet things such as nectar, they do not possess sucking mouthparts like bees, but have powerful jaws and a short tongue. They also differ from bees in that they feed their larvae on insects and scraps of carrion, rather than nectar and pollen. This wasp has just taken off from an apple to seek food elsewhere (above).

The **herbaceous border** is a colourful and nectar-rich part of the garden where geraniums, sedum, daisies, thistles and other plants thrive (right). On warm summer days, it is humming with insects, burying their heads in the flowers.

Earwigs spend much time curled up in flowers or crevices, emerging from time to time to feed, and often making holes in petals (below). Though rarely seen in flight, earwigs possess fan-like wings of great beauty.

The **large** or **cabbage white** (*Pieris brassicae*) used to be a serious pest in vegetable gardens, but due to decreasing numbers it no longer causes so much damage. A fully grown larva (above) feeds on a nasturtium flower, also a member of the cabbage family. An adult female shows her underwings (right), and (below) takes off from a curly kale leaf. In an effort to gain sufficient aerodynamic lift, the butterfly's wings are extended so far forward that they actually touch. (The insect is flying away from the camera.)

Another member of the white family, the **green-veined white** (*Pieris napi*), has settled on a bugle flower (right). The caterpillar of this butterfly does not destroy cabbages but, like the orange-tip butterfly, feeds on such plants as lady's smock and garlic mustard. The green-veined white is more attractive than the large white, being smaller with a dusting of green and yellow around the veins on the undersides of its wings.

Many kinds of true flies are attracted by flowers and fruits. Unlike butterflies, flies have short tongues so cannot extract nectar from thin, tubular flowers. Two very different types of fly are the attractively marked **hover fly** (*Helophilus pendulus*), seen here on a rose bloom (below), and a **flesh fly** which is drinking the surface juices of a ripe blackberry (bottom). There are numerous species of hover fly, most of which are beneficial as their larvae hunt greenfly, seizing them and sucking them dry. Flesh flies have somewhat unsavoury habits, spending their larval stage feeding on decaying animal matter as maggots. Even as adults they will imbibe the juices of putrefying bodies just as readily as blackberries.

An azalea bloom swarms with **green longhorns** (*Adela viridella*), tiny moths belonging to the Microlepidoptera (below). On warm spring days the males dance in courtship swarms high in the trees or in other spots which catch the sun, such as this bush. The larvae feed on the leaves of oak or birch, burrowing between the upper and lower surfaces.

Planting 'butterfly bushes' (*Buddleia davidii*) is one sure way of attracting many species of butterfly. Left alone, buddleias tend to have a rather brief flowering time, but with careful management it can be extended. Here two **peacocks** (*Vanessa io*) and two **small tortoiseshells** (*Aglais urticae*) are feasting on the copious quantities of nectar produced by the shrub. The mouthparts of insects vary, so different species can collect nectar from different types of flower. Butterflies and most moths have a long proboscis which enables them to reach down to the bottom of the long, narrow corolla tube for nectar.

As the larvae of both peacocks and small tortoiseshells feed on stinging nettles, growing 'controlled' patches of nettles is another way of encouraging these two butterflies to visit the garden.

On the wing, the pale-green female **brimstone** (*Gonepteryx rhamni*) is easily mistaken for its close relative the large white butterfly, but the brimstone has a somewhat stronger flight (above). The wings of this female, which has just taken off from a buddleia flower, are at the limit of a downstroke.

The name 'butterfly' originated with this lovely insect, which in medieval times was called 'butter-coloured-fly' as the males are sulphur-yellow in colour. Brimstones spend the winter hibernating in a thick clump of ivy or other evergreen bush, where their leaf-like wings blend with the surroundings. They are the first butterflies to appear in spring, waking up on the first warm days, sometimes as early as the end of February. Although it can be seen in gardens and open countryside, the brimstone is really a woodland butterfly.

After gathering nectar from a buddleia, a worker **honey bee** (*Apis mellifera*) leaves to visit another bloom nearby (right). A worker may fly huge distances to seek and bring home food to sustain the colony. Gradually its body loses its covering of hair, and its wings become ragged, and finally comes the flight from which it fails to return. In summer, worker bees live little longer than six weeks. Although they only forage in daylight and in reasonably good weather, activity within the hive never ceases.

Foxgloves (*Digitalis purpurea*), with their spikes of purple-spotted flowers and soft, downy leaves, occur naturally in scrub and open woodlands, particularly on acid soils; this clump has seeded itself at the edge of a heather bed (left). Wherever there are foxgloves there is the hum of foraging bumble bees, flying from one thimble-like flower to the next in their perpetual search for food.

Related to spiders, **harvestmen** (*Opiliones*) are characterized by their small, oval bodies and long, thin legs (right). Unlike spiders they are omnivorous, leaving their shelter under stones or amongst low vegetation to feed on vegetable matter, the remains of dead animals, and droppings, as well as hunting small invertebrates. Many species are nocturnal, but some can be found in daylight. This one is clambering around a foxglove in a shady corner of the garden.

Butterflies can be encouraged into the garden by cultivating both native and more exotic species of flowers, which should ideally be planted to produce a continuous supply of nectar through the summer. Heather may attract the **painted lady** (*Vanessa cardui*) (right). A **white admiral** (*Limenitis camilla*) (below) feeds on a blackberry flower. White admirals normally live and breed in deciduous forests with clearings or rides and honeysuckle for the larvae, so they are unlikely to visit gardens unless there is a suitable wooded habitat close by.

A **peacock** (*Vanessa io*) (right) has just taken off from knapweed. This butterfly is one of the few species to hibernate, usually in barns, sheds, hollow trees or suitably cool, dark corners indoors.

The **red admiral** (*Vanessa atalanta*) cannot survive the winter in cold climates as an adult, so recolonizes Europe from the south each spring (far right). A powerful flyer, it is well able to cross the Channel to Britain, and in autumn many red admirals which have bred in northern Europe make their way south again towards the Mediterranean, often flying at night. The caterpillars, like those of the peacock and small tortoiseshell, feed on stinging nettles.

When this garden was originally created in 1976, ecological factors were not considered at all; it was designed for ease of maintenance. Since then priorities have changed, even to the extent of incorporating a labour-intensive herbaceous border. But being surrounded by pastures, hedges, woodland and old farm buildings, there has never been a shortage of wildlife within its bounds.

The **small copper** (*Lycaena phlaes*) is particularly fond of the flowers of fleabane, a wild plant of the daisy family. The flight of coppers is rapid and erratic, making their course difficult to follow.

Like dragonflies, **hover flies** (*Syrphidae*) are capable of a bewildering range of aerial manoeuvres, including flying in any direction, rapid acceleration or hovering at a fixed point even in gusty conditions (above left). Hovering is mainly employed for courtship activities. The species here is *Syrphus balteatus*.

Both as adults and larvae, ladybirds prey on greenfly, aphids and scale insects, and so deservedly rank among the world's most beneficial insects. A single female may lay up to one thousand eggs, and with a life cycle of about four weeks and several broods a year, it is no wonder that they are so highly valued. A **seven spot ladybird** (*Coccinella 7-punctata*) searches for aphids on a rose (left).

Thistles, including the cultivated variety, are very popular with all sorts of insects, especially bumble bees (right). The bee seen here is a **carder bumble bee** (*Bombus agrorum*). On cold, wet and windy days when all other insects have long ceased to fly, it is the bumble bee which keeps going, visiting one bloom after another with dogged perseverance.

Grey squirrels (*Sciurus carolinensis*) are omnivorous rodents, feeding on fruit, nuts, seeds, shoots of trees and birds' eggs and young. Consequently, gardens cannot tolerate the destructive activities of too many squirrels, particularly during spring when birds are nesting. Fortunately, the few squirrels in this garden are only visitors from adjacent woodland and, apart from consuming most of the hazelnuts, they appear to do little damage. Squirrels do not hibernate but remain active throughout the winter, unless conditions are extremely severe, when they stay asleep in their dreys.

Evening

By evening plants are refreshed. They are very busy throughout the night as this is the time when they make new growth. Nutrients which were manufactured in sunlight by day are mobilized in the dark and used to build new cells. Each tiny new cell fills with water and is thus enlarged and strengthened. So the plant grows. This process can only take place in the cool of night when the plant is able to conserve sufficient water to sustain growth.

Even though their leaves are busily working, a few plants close their petals at dusk. Water lilies in the pond close up tightly at about 4 p.m. and actually sink into the water, leaving only the tips of their petals showing. It is as if they are determined to protect their pollen against the damp, cold night. Other flowers – the evening primrose, for example – open their petals as the light fades. These are invariably tubular flowers, like the tobacco plant, which provide nectar for night-flying moths and are dependent on these moths for pollination. White flowers are more visible as darkness falls; scentless mayweed, for example, takes on a more attractive appearance at dusk.

In the evening light a **blue tit** (*Parus caeruleus*) lands on a branch of corkscrew hazel before going to roost (right). The blue tit is really a woodland bird, but it can easily be encouraged to visit gardens regularly if nest boxes and suitable food at the bird-tray are provided.

The evening campion glows in the dark, but though visible to us it is not necessarily more visible to moths. It is a mistake to assume that other animals see the garden as we see it. Insects detect some colours and many also have an extended range of vision and are able to see in ultraviolet light. Just as many insects hear sounds that we cannot, so they see patterns on flowers that are not visible to us. The human eye recognizes colours but only when the light is bright; in the darkness everything appears in shades of grey. Mammals, on the other hand, do not have colour vision, but many can see in the dark.

As the setting sun glows red on the horizon everything begins to grow dim and colours fade. It is now that the garden is transformed. The air becomes fragrant as the night-scented stock opens its petals beneath the kitchen window. Fragrance in flowers is elusive – scented chemicals are usually oils which evaporate during the day. It is only in the cool air of evening, when the vapour condenses into tiny droplets, that the scent can be detected by our noses. The scent of honeysuckle is notably more delectable in the evening.

Night-flying moths seem able to discern the scent of flowers, which helps them in dim light. Their tiny eyes glow in the darkness like minute rubies and emeralds. Considering their highly successful adaptation to nocturnal life, it is curious that they are attracted to light, but many can be found clustering around lighted doorways and windows. Some of the larger hawk moths come out to feed in the evening, and rare moths, such as the canary-shouldered thorn, have been seen in the garden. Butterflies are resting by now. The comma settles quietly, resembling a dead leaf. As the shadows begin to lengthen, camouflage becomes more effective for many animals.

At this time, it is not uncommon to see the males of some insect species assembling to perform an aerial dance around the females. Crane flies, better known as daddy-long-legs, swarm in the early evening to perform their courtship dance. Many gnats, midges and, of course, mosquitoes dance, especially near the pond. By late summer the insect and spider population has increased vastly.

Hidden from view by day and protected from the drying sun by their shells, garden snails also increase in number during the summer. When the dew begins to settle in the evening they emerge from under the terrace steps and other hiding places. A snail moves on a broad muscular foot which is never in direct contact with the ground. It depends on a film of water on the ground because it glides on a secretion of slime which must not dry out. The glistening slime trail enables one to track the snail. Like many gastropods it has a homing instinct and will return to its

The **garden spider** (*Araneus diadematus*) is most likely to be seen in the centre of its web at night, as during daylight it usually remains under a leaf, hidden from diurnal predators. Orb-web spiders have a coating of oil on their legs which enables them to move rapidly over the sticky spirals without becoming trapped in their own snares.

base from a night's food foray, if it has time to do so before the morning sun dries out the dew. Warmth and humidity also encourage the toad to emerge. This is a useful animal to have in the garden as its rounded tongue is as efficient at catching insects as a frog's notched tongue. Toads crawl in a leisurely fashion and are less likely than frogs to leap or jump.

Early in the evening, while insects are still on the wing, swallows may be seen skimming across the garden, especially over the pond, and scooping up insects. They are accompanied in this laborious task by house martins and swifts, all of which need to supply hungry, fast-growing young with a protein-rich diet. Martins and swallows have become very dependent on man for nesting sites. Up at the house, martins paste their enclosed mud nests under the eaves. The swallows perch their open, more untidy nests on any shelf or ledge in the outhouses or barn. One has even succeeded in building on top of a lamp bracket. Apart from the pond which supplies mud for nests, the garden is of little interest to these birds, but they instinctively return to the same nesting sites year after year from places as far afield as South Africa.

As twilight closes in, silence descends: the familiar sounds of the day gradually diminish, birds stop twittering, the crickets quieten and the only disturbance is a rustling in the undergrowth. This is the time for owls to begin hunting. The barn owl, with its exceptionally soft and downy feathers, floats on silent wings. The tawny owl also hunts silently but its 'tu-whit, tu-whoo' has an eerie sound. Trees with hollows in the trunk accommodate the owls' nests.

Nearly all the small British mammals nest below ground level, the exceptions being the squirrel, dormouse and harvest mouse. Of the ground-dwellers that live in the garden it is the yellow-necked mouse that is most at home. It emerges at dusk from narrow runs under grass and leaf litter. Like the wood mouse it is not afraid to enter buildings and scuttles into the garden shed in search of stored apples.

Underground it must always seem like night and yet the animals of this dim, dark world do have a sense of day and night. Tunnelling just below the surface, a mole regularly causes havoc with the lawn. It is a solitary creature, living alone and feeding mainly on earthworms. On damp, dark evenings it pokes its highly sensitive snout above the surface and comes out to catch a slug or a snail. Not easy to catch and even more difficult to photograph, it retreats into its home with remarkable speed. Perhaps more irritating is the way it hastily throws up a heap of loose soil, barricading itself against further pursuit.

A **house mouse** (*Mus musculus*) stops briefly at the entrance of the stable before entering to look for meal pellets scattered on the floor by the horse.

Earthworm casts appear mainly on damp evenings and are not unlike miniature mole hills. Abundant in this garden, they are evidence of a fertile soil. Near the pond the rich black earth provides an ideal habitat for this unobtrusive underground dweller. The earthworm pulls dead leaves into its burrow, then eats and digests them. The undigested remains pass out leaving behind enriched, friable soil. Not only does it improve the quality of the soil by aerating it and by adding organic matter, the earthworm also buries quantities of dead plant material. It seems hard that such an industrious creature is often the first animal to be eaten in many food chains. However, as it is present in such large numbers, it can sustain considerable populations of other animals. It is a staple part of the diet of the garden fox, which is supplemented in summer by insects, in autumn by fruit and berries, and at opportune moments by the pickings of the dustbin.

As the moon rises, the garden can become strange, even a little sinister. This is the time that bats begin to fly and their sudden changes of direction in flight can be unnerving. Bats never come out on cold wet evenings, but on warm summer nights they begin to creep out of their crevices into the open roof space of the barn where they go through a ritual of vigorous grooming before flying out into the fading light. They hibernate in winter and are not seen again until late spring. Hedgehogs also hibernate but on a summer night it is easy to stumble over one crossing the lawn.

Daytime is always warmer than night, regardless of the season; it is during the evening that the temperature falls. Warm air over the house and garden rises and descending cool air takes its place. Birds can be seen taking advantage of this current of rising air to glide gracefully over the garden. Nocturnal moths are carried upwards; some are transported far from the garden, others drift in. The tiny dry fruits of some plants are equipped with parachutes of soft, fine bristles from which the seeds are suspended to delay their fall to the ground; on a summer evening the air is dotted with the floating parachutes of the dandelion. Falling fruits with helicopter wings spin and twirl as they descend from the parent tree; the maple tree depends on rising air currents to turn tiny propellers that carry its seeds away.

Sometimes the rising air, known as a thermal, is laden with moisture. The air cools as it rises and water vapour condenses into tiny drops, forming clouds which look like puffs of cotton wool in the evening sky. Occasionally these produce a gentle shower of rain, refreshing after the dryness of a hot day.

A well-designed **terrace** helps to connect the house to the garden (right). It is also a good place to observe wildlife. During the day a variety of creatures may be seen; the flowers are humming with insect life, while wrens search for insects amongst the vegetation. At night wood mice scuttle about looking for crumbs or other food put out for the birds, and occasionally a hedgehog may be glimpsed in the twilight hunting for slugs and snails.

As the fall gets under way, a mosaic of dying **leaves** of assorted colours and shapes collects on the pond's surface before decaying and sinking (overleaf).

Many creatures, from snails and spiders to toads and wrens, hide away in the thick mat of vegetation which envelops these **brick steps** (left).

Each night during summer a large **common toad** (*Bufo bufo*) ventures out from its hiding place in the wall to catch insects which have been attracted to the outside light (below). The common toad is the largest and most widespread European amphibian. Old females may reach six inches in length and almost the same in width when they inflate themselves. Toads are intelligent creatures and easily tamed. They are particular about their choice of pond for breeding. In spring they return *en masse* to their ancestral spawning pond, often travelling a mile or so, and ignoring other patches of water on the way.

As autumn drifts in, spent leaves float to the ground to return to the dust from which they sprang. The colourful fallen leaves of this **Norway maple** (*Acer platanoides*) will soon fade as bacteria and fungi start the process of decay (below).

A stroboscopic flash catches a **seed** of the Norway maple as it spirals to the ground (right).

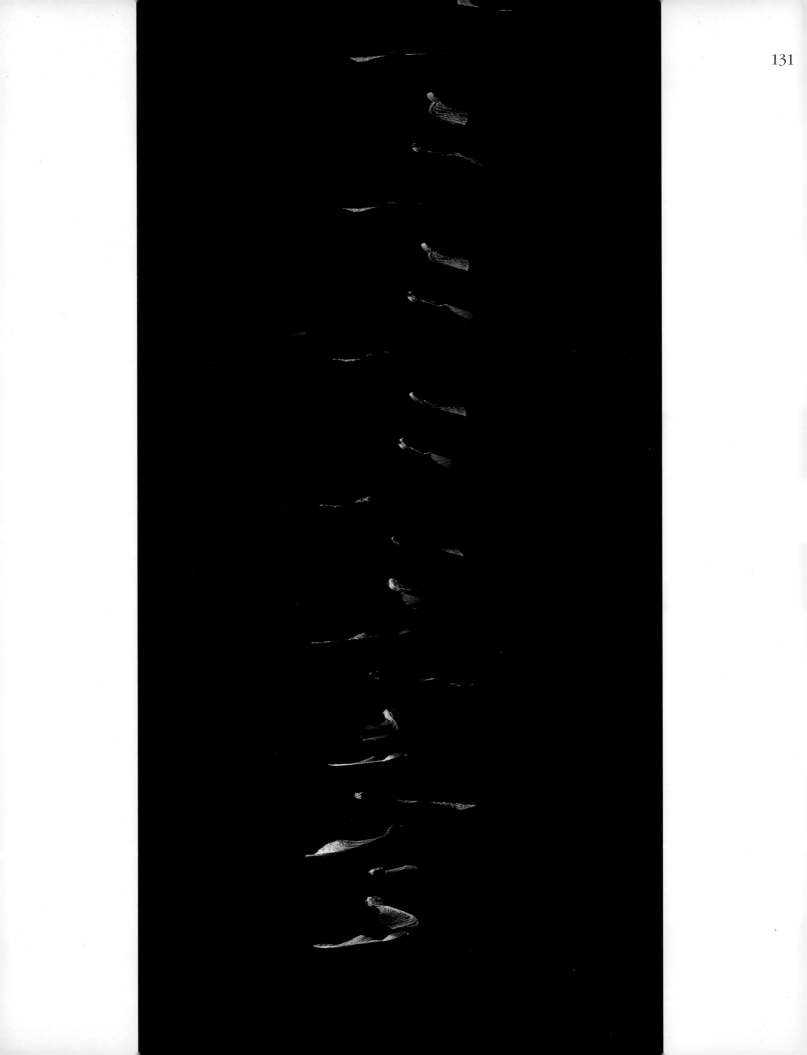

132

Bush crickets (family *Tettigonidae*) live in trees and bushes and have long, whip-like antennae (left). The female has a conspicuous sword-like ovipositor with which she inserts her eggs into the tissues of plants. Bush crickets feed on a wide variety of plant and animal matter. This green species has been feeding on the pollen of evening primrose.

Jumping spiders do not rely on webs to ensnare their prey. They walk in a series of jerks, and when they spot an insect with their battery of eyes, they stalk it as stealthily as a cat and leap on to the victim's back. Some species can jump up to twenty times their body length.

The **zebra spider** (*Salticus scenicus*) is our most familiar species, as the walls and fences of houses and gardens are among its favourite hunting grounds (below). It is most often seen in the daytime, but if warm enough it will remain active well into the evening.

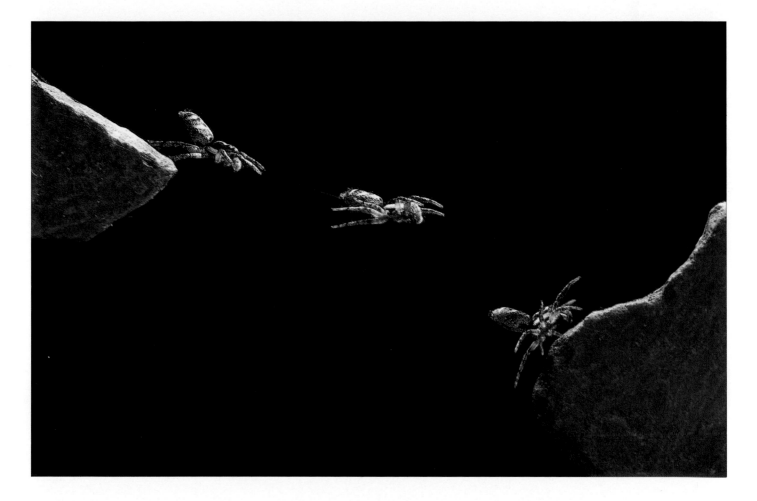

After a late evening visit to feed its young, a **jackdaw** (*Corvus monedula*) leaves its nest hole in the barn wall. Jackdaws usually nest in small colonies, in holes of trees, cliffs or ruined buildings. They frequently feed with rooks, from which they can be distinguished by their smaller size, shorter bill and patch of grey at the back of the head. Jackdaws are intelligent and active, often performing aerobatics for no apparent reason.

Although originally a woodland bird, the **blackbird** (*Turdus merula*) has now adapted very successfully to a life in parks and gardens, even in the middle of towns. It is often heard before it is seen, singing, scolding or uttering its extended alarm call, or noisily turning over dead leaves. Blackbirds also like fruit, especially berries; this one is having a late feed on the yellow berries of a cotoneaster before settling down for the night.

Before the countryside was cluttered with houses, **swallows** (*Hirundo rustica*) must have nested in caves or hollow trees. Nowadays they prefer to rear their young inside buildings, particularly barns and outhouses. They usually construct their mud-cup nest on a beam or rafter, but this one (above) has chosen a light fitting in an old stable. (See also page 147.)

Living and roosting in the same loft as the barn owl are several pairs of **white doves** (left). It may seem surprising to find these two very different birds living with one another so peacefully, but as one is active at night and the other during the day, their paths only cross at twilight when they occasionally meet face to face on the barn ledge.

Heather beds are very worthwhile additions to the garden. Apart from looking attractive throughout the year and requiring minimum maintenance, **heathers** are very popular with all sorts of insects, particularly bees and butterflies, which visit the ever-changing, colourful blooms from early spring to late autumn.

Diving through an opening high up in the barn, a **barn owl** (*Tyto alba*) enters with a mouse to feed its three hungry owlets (left). To see this magnificent bird quartering a meadow in the twilight, drifting low and ghost-like on silent wings in its search for mice and voles, is an unforgettable experience. Barn owls prefer to hunt over open countryside, relying on their superb hearing to locate prey. They do not visit gardens as a rule, unless there is a suitable nesting site or hunting area nearby.

Over the last few decades the barn owl has been becoming rare due to loss of habitat, pollution and collision with cars. When we really begin to treat the countryside more gently, and this bird's haunts are restored, then the tide may turn in its favour.

Away from the barn owls, in the relative safety of the garden shed, a **yellow-necked mouse** (*Apodemus flavicollis*) has discovered the apple store (below). Like the wood mouse, this similar but slightly bigger species is largely nocturnal and is frequently an uninvited guest in houses during autumn.

This golden-yellow **stagshorn fungus** (*Calocera viscosa*) is growing around some rotting larch logs in a damp corner (left). It is more commonly found arising from buried roots and old stumps in coniferous woods.

Growing in the soil of a disused flower pot is a cluster of **liverworts** (*Marchantia polymorpha*) (below). These dark-green plants produce male and female structures or 'gemmae' during spring and summer; the male parts are disc-like, while the female parts resemble miniature palm trees, having about nine spreading fingers. Liverworts are related to mosses and made up of flat, lobed structures with no conventional roots. They reproduce by means of spores.

Robins (*Erithacus rubecula*) will nest almost anywhere, including hedges, banks, shrubs, the ground, old machinery, tin cans or, in this case, a shelf in the garden shed (above). The average lifespan of a robin is only about a year, but if luck is on their side they can survive for as long as ten years. In Britain the robin is the national bird, and those living in parks and gardens often become very tame. In Europe they are rather more secretive and difficult to observe.

Green lacewings (*Chrysopa* sp.) fly both during the day and at night, and with their large, flimsy, net-like wings of bluish-green, they are easily distinguished from other insects (right). They play an important part in the ecology of gardens since, like ladybirds, both the adults and larvae feed on aphids. They frequently come into the house or garden shed to hibernate during autumn, when they lose their lovely colour and turn a dull brown.

Every year a pair of **swallows** (*Hirundo rustica*) nests in a stable next to the barn. As the fledglings get older they consume so much food that the parent birds have to sweep in and out of the stable door every minute or so with beakfuls of insects caught on the wing.

Several centuries ago, when all the swallows mysteriously vanished in autumn, it was thought that they flew to the moon. We now know that most fly to South Africa, to return again in April. The nest and young of this bird appear on page 137.

The **pipistrelle** (*Pipistrellus pipistrellus*) is the smallest and most numerous European bat. It is also a very active one, snapping up flies and small moths which it catches on the wing in its tail pouch. During the day it roosts in a crevice of a tree, wall or roof of a house. Pipistrelles give birth to a single baby, which is able to fly within a month.

Considering how lethargically the **common toad** (*Bufo bufo*) proceeds on foot, it comes as a great surprise to see it catch prey. The bulbous tongue shoots out of the gaping mouth, envelops its victim, in this case a worm, and is withdrawn in a flash. If the prey is large enough, the toad may use its 'hands' to cram the remainder into its mouth. Toads have an enormous appetite, and experience no difficulty in enjoying a continual feast. Their diet consists of any living creature they can swallow.

In the evening, when conditions are sufficiently damp, a **common garden snail** (*Helix aspersa*) ventures out from its daytime haunt under the wall to find some tender young shoots. A wildlife garden would be a poorer place without slugs and snails, as so many creatures, including thrushes and hedgehogs, rely on them as a major source of food. All land snails are hermaphrodite and have a bizarre courtship ritual which involves injecting calcareous darts into one another.

Unlike other crows, the **jay** (*Garrulus glandarius*) rarely flies into the open, so it is a difficult bird to observe for long. Usually all one sees of this shy and restless bird is a rear view of pinkish-brown feathers as it disappears into the foliage. Jays are extremely noisy, and their loud and usually twice-repeated rasping shrieks of alarm are often the first and only sign of their presence.

As darkness falls, moths wake and leave their daytime hiding places. Here a **canary-shouldered thorn** (*Deuteronomous alminaria*) arouses, having spent the day simulating a fallen leaf on an old fence (below).

The **barn owl** (*Tyto alba*) hunts mainly at night, but when food is in short supply in winter, or when it is feeding young, it may be seen hunting during the early evening or even in the middle of the day (right). Barn owls are not the most vocal of owls, but are capable of producing hissing and snoring sounds as well as occasional long, eerie shrieks.

In rural areas **foxes** (*Vulpes vulpes*) have always entered gardens at night to find food (left), but recently, in response to changing conditions, they have not only moved into towns, but have become far less nocturnal, prowling around in daylight, particularly when there are cubs to feed.

The adaptability of this handsome and successful mammal is also demonstrated by its flexible feeding habits. Though in the country it preys mostly on birds, eggs, insects and small mammals, in built-up areas, it will scavenge on almost anything. This fox is rummaging around a dustbin in the back yard.

Another scavenger, but one which has been following man around for centuries, is the **brown rat** (*Rattus norvegicus*), seen here leaping from a dustbin (below). Like so many scavengers, it is highly successful, thriving in a variety of habitats from farmyards, gardens and warehouses to city sewers and rocky shores. Brown rats breed prodigiously, with litters of up to twelve produced at four-week intervals.

Sadly, bats are becoming increasingly rare, but the **common long-eared bat** (*Plecotus auritus*) is more frequently seen than most other species (right). A lover of woodland, it usually hunts for insects on foliage, flying slowly and often hovering to pick them off leaves. As well as employing echolocation for hunting insects on the wing, the long-eared bat can locate prey passively. Like the barn owl which listens for rodents on the ground, this bat can detect insects rustling amongst the foliage.

During the day, long-eared bats roost upside-down in hollow trees, and if we are fortunate, in the lofts of our houses.

It can be quite daunting to meet a male **stag beetle** (*Lucanus cervus*) flying through the dusk with a sinister buzzing of wings (below). Stag beetles survive where there are rotting oak stumps, so the urge of many foresters and gardeners to clear away old and fallen trees does little to encourage this and many other creatures which rely on decaying wood for their existence.

Notes on the Photography

A wide variety of approaches and photographic techniques were adopted to tackle the range of subjects and habitats portrayed in this book. These involved the use of different cameras, daylight, flash and both field and studio locations.

With the exception of safari holiday photography, when one 'shoots from the hip' from within a vehicle, most serious nature photography requires some understanding of the subject, an appreciation of lighting, patience and, in most situations, only a limited knowledge of photography. These days cameras have 'auto-everything', and nine times out of ten produce acceptably exposed and focused pictures. This only really applies when working in the field, however, where nature controls the subject, background and lighting. Photography in the studio is another matter altogether, requiring not only comprehensive technical know-how and mastery of lighting, but an in-depth knowledge of the natural history and behaviour of the subject in front of you, particularly with regard to setting and choice of background. Generally, studio work also demands even more patience, and consummate attention to detail; unfortunately, it is rarely as exciting as working in the wild.

The large majority of the photographs here were taken in or around the garden and farm buildings surrounding my house; the remainder were taken in studio settings. An entertaining exercise for those sufficiently moved would be to try to tell them apart – they should be indistinguishable, even to expert naturalists or photographers!

Approximately two-thirds of the photographs were taken on 35mm format, and one-third on 2¼ inch square. In all cases the cameras were set on 'auto-nothing', when aperture, shutter speed and focusing were adjusted manually. Cameras used were Nikon F4 equipped with lens focal lengths from 28mm to 500mm, and Hasselblad with lenses from 50mm to 150mm. All the exposures were made on Kodachrome or Fuji Velvia reversal material, both of which are slow, high resolution emulsions.

Daylight was used as a sole light source for exposing about half of the photographs, while flash was necessary for the remainder – again, in many instances, it should be difficult or impossible to tell them apart. Flash is indispensable when working at night or in the dark, or where rapid movement needs to be arrested. To freeze the high-speed activities of insects, birds and other creatures, special flash equipment was employed with a speed of about 1/20,000th of a second, together with the associated electronic gadgets for detecting the animal at the right moment and firing the shutter.

A sturdy tripod was used to support the camera for every photograph.

Index